DISORDER

Concetta Principe

Jan 30/25

Copyright © 2024 Concetta Principe

All rights reserved. No part of this work may be reproduced or used in any form, except brief passages in reviews, without prior written permission of the publisher.

Edited by Shane Neilson
Cover and book design by Jeremy Luke Hill
Proofread by Carol Dilworth
Set in PT Mono, Open Sans, and Linux Libertine
Printed on Mohawk Via Felt
Printed and bound by Arkay Design & Print

LIBRARY AND ARCHIVES CANADA CATALOGUING IN PUBLICATION

Title: Disorder / Concetta Principe.
Names: Principe, Concetta, author.
Description: Poems.
Identifiers: Canadiana (print) 20230580424 | Canadiana (ebook) 20230580432 | ISBN 9781774221068 (softcover) | ISBN 9781774221082 (EPUB) | ISBN 9781774221075 (PDF)
Subjects: LCGFT: Poetry.
Classification: LCC PS8581.R5512 D57 2024 | DDC C811./54—dc23

Gordon Hill Press gratefully acknowledges the support of the Canada Council for the Arts, the Ontario Arts Council, and the Ontario Book Publishing Tax Credit.

Gordon Hill Press respectfully acknowledges the ancestral homelands of the Attawandaron, Anishinaabe, Haudenosaunee, and Métis Peoples, and recognizes that we are situated on Treaty 3 territory, the traditional territory of Mississaugas of the Credit First Nation.

Gordon Hill Press also recognizes and supports the diverse persons who make up its community, regardless of race, age, culture, ability, ethnicity, nationality, gender identity and expression, sexual orientation, marital status, religious affiliation, and socioeconomic status.

Gordon Hill Press
130 Dublin Street North
Guelph, Ontario, Canada
N1H 4N4
www.gordonhillpress.com

Table of Contents

RUNNING FROM THE SUNSHINE OF MY LIFE — 1

BASEMENT
WROUGHT — 9
THE SUBLIME — 10
CUT LILACS — 11
SAD THIGHS — 12
MIRACLES — 18
WHERE TO GO — 19
CATCH 22 — 20
A Tree Bath — 21

CAKE AS PARADIGM
ONE — 25
PARTY FAVOURS — 26
SEAM — 27
ICING ON THE CAKE — 28
ANOREXIA — 29
PARANOIA — 30

KITCHEN
IF THIS KITCHEN COULD TALK — 35
HOW TO BE RUDE — 37
THE ANOREXIC — 38

ROOM
I HAVE A THEORY — 43
A LETTER TO THE FUTURE WITHOUT SNOW — 45
BLUE — 47
WHERE ARE — 48
WAS THERE — 49
NABATEAN BEAUTY — 50

WINDOW
BPD (A PREFACE TO A PORTRAIT)	55
PORTRAITS OF A HIGH FUNCTIONING BORDERLINE PERSONALITY DISORDER	56
SUBJECTIVE DESTITUTION	75
Notes and Acknowledgements	77
About the Author	78

"I run among the ruins"
 - Anne Carson

RUNNING FROM THE SUNSHINE OF MY LIFE

I her witness as she rolls in, screaming
through the streets

sliding under cars, over
hats, into crevices, right

at me. I cling to the dark side of maples shuttering
my ears making you all turn

wondering
what has gotten into me.

when she leaves, I grind
the remnants of her

glossy red evening gown into
the fleas of my fury

dreaming
she knows

how it feels.

I, her Picasso's missing black period
I, her cubist crushing

antimatter. I
her mortal shade

the eclipse that will
devour her

but for now, she is Shirley Temple and that
outdated, with precocious curls

and dimples to seduce me
from my grave, as if

who does she think she is, parading
in her hydrogen chains

through the trees, picking
columbine, loving squirrels?

drenching
me in burning

summer when the night
is too short before she comes again

splashing acid sweetness
that folds, half by half

till winter shortens her

radiant decibels to
sad fractions, easing

my nerves.

she pours through doors and runs
along the carpets, wood floors, spilling

into backyard barbecues
and birthday cakes

what a mess: and still you turn
to soak her up: can't you hear

the poison of her two-faced radiance?
she is the alpha to omega

of crimes against humanity she
is a weapon of disease

cancer, melanoma, heat
she screams

and you take the blame. don't you hear
her

so effing loud
my head aches?

she gets up from her diurnal
fall, radiant and honoured for dropping

wave after wave of her perfume
of light cutting through the smog

of bad thoughts. Give me a break.
She's no Prozac guys, she's

selfish,
toxic,

indiscriminate,
self-aggrandizing,

her role

as mother of all
life:

obviously a megalomaniac

you are all
caught in her cult,

turning when she does, rising
and sleeping

to her circadian rule, smile
when she does. she has

wrapped you round
her proverbial

finger but I am
the thumb

of her truth.
the curtain

of her
tomorrow

the sum

BASE MENT

WROUGHT

blue hand of a girl
spread cool

to a fault, running down
cornflowers sequined along time's highway

wrought by Queen Anne's lace
with summer

bangs in every corner
of the quarry

where mom's silver
healed sling-backs

slipped
from the basement of her reach

sort of like a song

THE SUBLIME

but a dream

radiant
awesome

and life darkened after that, dragged
to the knees, landing

midway down the stairs
shadowing yards

of purple wool in the skirt, pounds of chocolate
on the cheeks, scissors, paper, rock

she couldn't say it, that she was
in bed with sorrow

its pigment stinking
chiaroscuro sheets

hung by hopscotch in the trees

CUT LILACS

to slide
down the basement

stairs, wings
of concrete

guarding the base
note of twilight

blue, while the pencil rasping
at the sheets

the plumbing
rushing overhead

cut lilacs
to their knees

SAD THIGHS

Like Emily who bound
her disorder to her last

reclusive poet years, wearing
walls of her room as a plaster

hijab, anachronistically applied
here

she veils herself with brick
and mortar

on foundations
that weep

cries

of don't desert me
to herself she cries

at the atom
of history

cries a four-year-old girl
on the street

fumbling after mom
striding away

cry the flowers

eyeing pairs
on the dance floor

the widening of their
wild, the shaming

of their sidelong
glances at her hanging at the wall

stuck with a pin
of paranoia

why is it so so easy
for them?

mitigating

grief
by taking a jackhammer

to the bad
cracks, this is her rage shining

through the windows
cutting the meat

for the cat looking
for a way out

she is
saddled

with internal
umwelt

the flea its soul
she can't shake

scratching
at depression

lice across her anxiety
it all looks the same

this home that never
had her back, anyway, forget

room for what she was

symptom

of what is nowhere
near yard enough, nor deep

enough, no sky thunder
enough, no alley

kind enough, no tree
tender enough

in a neighbourhood
unzoned for her monstrous

sad thighs

MIRACLES

For all the boundless
time we have to plan

advance
second by second
towards dinner

for all our apparent freedom
to cut fruit or broil
turnips for the stew

moving, or bending
as we want and reaching

with the spoon into
this bowl

for all this mobility we suppose
the truth is we

are
stone eating walls

time laughs at us her miracles
look there

a mountain moved, a dragon died,
a broken leg

WHERE TO GO

In the second half of life there is

a second prison
locking you into

footings tolerating mud
memories, failures that stick

collectively thick
as despond

painful and bunioned failures
masticating cud

of identity fondue, here

water levels are rising
up to your eye

balls here

you are the real
under
ground

recusing yourself
knowing

where you stand—

from down here
you can tell the ableists what is holding

them up, and where
to go

CATCH 22

    am I
    too old to catch your ear?
    too slow with metaphors?
    too personal to inspire your interest, my personal not being
        your hard on? talking woman's hard on, too, here.
    lacking pheromones in my tears?

    am I
    not androgenized enough, or not as fluid as I should be? or too
        full, bloated and shapeless?

    am I
    barking up the wrong Tree, Clorinda?

    am I
    too old, Clorinda?
    a mule in a cattle field?
    spluttering "Marcia, Marcia, Marcia" Brady?

    am I
    so out of pace, you don't hear me, not even my ticks?
    anachronistic, contributing to ancient detritus?
    so mould you're sick?
    so unwantable you've forgotten to ghost me?

    am I
    really only that, worthless sagging tits, menopause waist and
        wrinkled hips, faceless, voiceless, relic of a vessel? or
        should I have killed myself last century so you can
        drink my blood for breakfast

    fresh blood or dead feminist for you champions?

A Tree Bath

us wood dragons
are baptized by birth

N O choice in the matter
no point in regretting

that all this wonderful Material of us
can't be cut Down to make your house.

too late. that's right we have been made
paper thin as the walls

from being punched into a pulp
and thrown in the bleach bath

another baptism but the one
that kills us for our resurrection

pressed into a
trompe l'oeil

of wallpaper
with black sparks

of our rancor
plastering

the walls
surrounding your

throne rolled dull
as that sceptre

by your side something
to think about next

time you wipe

CAKE AS PARADIGM

ONE

the lilac roots completely

out of season and the dandelion
friends foreshadowing

winter sun
through the kitchen window

on the skirts of a girl's furious hunger
so heavy she sits cross-legged

on green and white
squares of linoleum dressed

in daisies made
to ladder

the chair to her sister's birthday cake
one candle

handled
with the skill of an HB eraser

PARTY FAVOURS

she thorns
the day of self

pity at the age of six playing
catch up to the screaming

stick of the tail on the ass
of a donkey dress torn in the tree

of a three-legged race
that her sister takes, the way she

took the best shirt, the first
slice of her birthday

cake and maybe stole her wish
oh to wish

to just melt away

SEAM

As if
she isn't there

when passing
on the stair of Jacob's

laddering her basement
sewing room, she can hear

a pin drop between the cool,
blue hands

ripping
stitches

of this deer
skin dotted

with machine gun holes
candling the arm pit

of this coat
of a birthday

ICING ON THE CAKE

Just so you know knots
are the pyrotechnics of appetite

repressant; a kink in the intestine
of this birthday cake

wrapped in frosted lake; fired
up candles a flambe

of generations dressed
with wound calories. why not

blame the complex sodiums creams
cheese whiz starched

collars al
Gaudi, this day

born of
layered revenge

cold and no re-
treat

ANOREXIA

Dirt this pitcher
dig this

girth
with debt, denting

off excess, the skirting
plodding dishrag

worn chiffon
or crepe

caved
social storms

a pelvis, a cloak, a pose

get under, sleep in
your angel food, give

shame for free
to the first bush

growing treacle
fishcake, upside down

a birthday cake
a patty cake

lake and bread
laine, lone

naked
life

PARANOIA

Too many eyes on
this, too many

judges slaying my
dragons, too many

looks of contempt
forcing underground

everything
you cannot read is here

undercover
desperate

for oxygen choking
on my insides

much as an anorexic
eats herself

KIT
CHEN

IF THIS KITCHEN COULD TALK

It would be a woman
walking out the door

one who whistled
while the kitchen dressed

the salad pink to match
her skirt

ballooning by the sink, a Marilyn
posed and ditsy, thus dishing

chicken talk and twisted
necks, sandwich, salt, prefix

homework on the table
sexed fowl

baking, towelling
the crying on the floor

walls slippery with participle
now duodecimal

sodium spoiling
the worm

for science, stop you're whining eat
your chicken stop your playing

and he ate everything on the plate, one
thing at a time

while adults drama
over beef bourguignon

these walls do not have ears
anymore, they have

speech marks, sharp, cruel, tagged
and indecent

HOW TO BE RUDE

Let me eat the peace
between us, bitter sauce, the detente

of a war of eggs over easy, toasting
sweaty granules

of word after word, not that I don't want
to eat the delicate scramble

of purple parsley, those paisley laws
of your sartorial trauma

because when I eat
your chocolate knights

of sonnets, each verbal morsel of
sauteed articles'

particular
blame then I, dear

Shakespeare of our modern age
with your torpedo

torment
in the chef's reduction

of love, I

feast on nothing.
I'm sorry: was that rude?

THE ANOREXIC

starch the steak, pepper
the park before you

plate my daughter's footwear
Fluevog never tasted as good

as those wedding
Bombanieries

rutty candy wrapped
in ribbon tied

with thanks for your money
put on your

gold shoes, hour the minutes
then splice

each second thin enough
to paper cut

your hand
five seconds

is all you need

ROOM

I HAVE A THEORY

I am a child in the basement of life looking up at the sky through the window from the back seat of the car, believing we are low flying birds

A childish fantasy of an abduction movie. I want to speak to the notion of fantasy because I think I know Lacan's theory of fantasy, because theoretically, one day, I will Finnegan Wake the master off the stage

I am long on thought and small on drawing wide at the table with good fat legs, see me stand and roar four (that was not a comma splice, but this is. grammar theory. fragment.)

I am marking and marking and my blood feels written all over with the thoughts of these young people who don't know what they're doing, anguished, raw, affect

Power in them

I theorize and prioritize and theoretically speaking follow Derrida in his there and not here, or is that Stein on the theory of what is poetry what is prose and there there is no there, there

Stein's theory was that question marks were redundant ?? and the comma

I have a theory I have too many theories stemming from my first which was all about birds and how their hearts beat to the urban rhythm

Fast was how I set the metronome to represent modernity ricocheting off the curtain walls, birds breaking their necks on humanity, in theory, glass hangs, a shudder but nothing shatters

I really did I, didn't I, Derrida whose aleph is a formula for Lacan's everything

I will is a theory of time, Shakespeare, Nietzsche's basement of founding fathers from which the Uberman shall leap,

the corners of the world are four, the earth's crust is time sensitive, and therein my theory circles the catacombs of patriarchy, my childhood in a bath with rubber ducks that roar, in theory,

I go on and can't and move on the flying failure theme of Beckett's clock and Pie

proves infinity
etc.

A LETTER TO THE FUTURE WITHOUT SNOW

the snow of an urban bread, bodied and laced by vehicular coughing and streetcar bells in the atmosphere. streets thickening with boots kneading at winter's blanket. stop the street light just by watching it. can you imagine?

do you have a coldness that is not black, where you are? does gravity treat your depression differently than it does for us here? can you change the stars just by looking at them?

do you see sky in your dreams? I mean, do you dream in colour or is it all black sky, white light? me I dream of flying. because awake, I am so pedestrian, inching on the smart map in my hand. get lost, never. do you feel loss of space, or lost in outer space? no star to reach in your lifetime, I suppose. we are an ant burning on the sun.

I imagine you are an ancient ship, in the wrong century. or a boat in winter streets. I guess you can't spin your wheels the way kids do here, roaring through Cape Cod summer castles, crashing into NY towers. I guess you discard the past as arcane, and the future already here.

do you have traffic jams out there? can you spend a lifetime watching two stars collide? must be boring, after a while. what about your senses are like ours? do you have windows: I mean, are you sensitive to the soul of the universe and the snow inside the one you love?

I imagine a hill of wintered wooliness snowshoed at the blue hour, while you sleep beneath your thin thermal layers, shedding dreams of dog—

do you have dogs where you are? do the dogs remember who they are, Huskies or the Samoyeds? do you feel them yearn for home there, just as they do here, when ploughing through the winter storm to the fire and food they left behind? do you dream of fire? can you dream at all?

me, I dream of being a future puddle holding a place in the sun, one foot and a leg disappearing the dark skys—

BLUE

Not dark but dusk red, blue lies all over the place. not hiding in the close walls of delight, dusted, scattered bright. childhood blue runs everywhere and her four-eyes in grade two, bleeding math with sky writing. a plane overhead. her family is in it, which was not a lie when she thought it. so many childhoods in a litter box. so many infantile abandons and schisms, fantastic drawings on shitty paper, long forgotten bruises, incisions. a lot of math. little blue chips from the cat's eye and cradle. see that? tomatoes long and pretty on the floor, peach to red. meanwhile, blue falls. blue in the folds, little lies of gold. long shirt and short pants. come away from that periodic table. come away with me. chemistry is poetry but what we need is math. a long view of engineering a child's disorder. crying in the playground because the plane was heading to Italy, and her family was in it, without her. that memory, plural as the blue skies, was not a lie when she thought it.

WHERE ARE

Where are your lips as you read this do you follow me the way my father follows English in *The Globe* or any newspaper mouthing the words to slow the river of letters, quietly humming as if in prayer, each vowel and phoneme and muscular silent 'ough', like Nichol's 'daughter in slaughter', what about laughter, dipthongs and silent 't's of listening? Lis-ten to me. Or lately, K-nife. K-night. K-nih-gt.

The silent colours that collect around a field in winter.

You need the horizon to know what I mean.

Vast wintered field at Downsview hangar rising up from where the boys are playing soccer on Saturday night.

The up of sky and the thick overhang of cloud, let me say about that

Let me me say that this day day is everything that world that world has an up up and down it has this, this let me say is the gravity of that matter

Do you follow me, up the down and then down under the great hole of this pome-granite?

WAS THERE

ever a thirty years ago? was there. ever anything other than sitting on that patio in your summer dress trying to finish the screen play? even then, was a season ever worn through? was there

a reason to eat eggs, instead? over easy please. was there skin before this tarnished silver, delicate as rice paper? our writing. what about coffee? was there another chance to start that memoir? if there was a chance to write this, was there

everything necessary in these thirty years? long drinking through short nights till dawn and crashing. there was a promise and many promises. there was the memoir not yet written. there was never a draft, more eggs over easy, but there was vision. was there a way to write it before the end? you wanted to give hope by writing after cancer. was there a more compelling reason to wait? your chapped lips, water there was there

ever a chance to start? thirty years ago, there was never a question. just Dooney's, coffee, dreams still fresh and a new project to finish. was there a day without cancer. yes, you say in my head: yes.

every woman was there

sad and unfinished things of thirty years. and I am harping on your unmade memoir. the painting I made you: "Hold it till I'm back." will you come back? I hear your regrets. I want you here, writing. was there a chance? goddamn it, was there

ever a chance to write before the end?

For Andrea Moodie, 1964-2020.

NABATAEAN BEAUTY

I met an American who married the guide who led her through Petra. Prince Charles was guided to take Diana as his bride.

Petra was built by the Nabataeans. don't be fooled by their sense of design. they had a lot of skill in carving but probably used the dirt for a throne and hands, their table.

the emptiness of beauty is not an ancient proverb, but a place where you can walk the palatial valley, royal envy. absolute hollow, a kind of alcohol-free vodka.

the echo chamber of a glass, goblet, gun, cell, all these hollows, sleepy even. for the Nabataeans, the face of it was the point.

a face as flat as paper, bent here and there to fake depth. can we even blame the artisans who were probably too tired to go deeply into character? can we blame them for our disappointment in discovering that, passing the monstrous doorway with its pillars and carvings, we are in a dark cave with a fire pit in the centre?

I wonder if this is how Lady Di felt about her marriage: a dress with nothing in it.

WINDOW

"I am out with lanterns, looking for myself"
—Emily Dickinson

BPD (A PREFACE TO A PORTRAIT)

I am the invisible cloak which is why
no-no one will take

me from me, not being able
to see what I am

I am human passing as this tacky
swatch of fur; so shag purple

I can't fall, and when I tumble
from my post on the wall

—someone hung me there
for a joke— I make

a sound of crashing
the invisible cloak

against my arm
thwack

to pronounce
my absence

I admit I was once
human passing

for who I am

PORTRAITS OF A HIGH FUNCTIONING BORDERLINE PERSONALITY DISORDER

Because, as she will have explained to the CAMH psychiatrist when the diagnosis session begins, she knows she has a disorder. When she is given the reigns and the future is hers, she loses her grip. It's a physical feeling of psychic weakness. A kind of carpal tunnel syndrome of will. Her nerves feel cut off so she can't hold on, so she spins away in the 2001 universe. But then there looms another chance at Jupiter in the void and she leaps. In short, she has spent her life recursively leaping from one silent opportunity of unearthly proportions to another. Trying not to get caught by entropy. Trying but failing to find her proper orbit. Holding tight until the psychic syndrome un-ables her again.

Borderline Personality Disorder (BPD) is what you make when you're too young to know anything different.

1. BORDERS

BPD. This psychic house without borders, forget defining them as good and bad. Or perhaps those borders are red lines that get crossed, again and again, back and forth, so that in the end all that's left is an ugly maroon stain of Raggedy Anne executions. A kind of cutting away, you see, of the things she loves.

She says fuck you to the psychiatric community and not just because her mother was a psychiatric social worker, who of all people would have recognized her behaviour as symptoms of the condition. Can't blame her mother, though, since not one of the countless psychiatric professionals has reached out across this abyss separating her from the world to say: this is who you are, let me help you live with it.

Instead, she did as all undiagnosed people do: self-medicate, self-regulate, self-loath and, for the most part, fake being normal. And she found a thing to hold on to for dear life. That thing was her desk, in metaphorical terms; in literal terms, it was writing.

In two weeks a psychiatrist will put her under the analysand microscope, prodding her with the questions that will explain her bad self-image, her failures, her fear of attachment which is understood as abandonment, even after 23 years of marriage, her failure to bond with others or her faulty judgment in impulsive action, her inner bleak darkness that no one should see because how could one live with it? Her self-harm and her not eating. Her inconsistency, shifting from depressed to sometimes functioning. Which is she: a mad person or neurotic? Wild is that the psychiatrist will laugh at her joke ("CAMH is a joke") as if he is not surprised by that, that her humour cuts the loaf to the sour truth. As if knowing full well that humour is not necessarily a sign of health.

Her carpal tunnel syndrome of will, her border crossing. She went to almost every school in the city, breaking boundaries of public school caches. She got along with classmates well enough, but nothing gelled. Rarely after school time. All her drama played out in the privacy of her mind: couldn't be sure she was saying what she meant, she couldn't reach out, she dissociated. Not finding the attention she needed, she leapt into another school district. Maybe that's why she never held on or, you might say, they let go. Her first experiences of floating off, a body in 2001, spinning from universe to universe. In fundamental terms, comparatively friendless.

But to be fair, she has friends today, whom she loves; and they are friends because they stick around and agree to live by her rules which are never explicitly defined: she loves them, and thinks about them, but just doesn't reach out. She is a passive entity, responding to good will but sure of being brushed off, she initiates little.

2. ABANDONMENT ISSUES

Abandonment is the greatest anxiety: better to be alone than to be cut off from humanity. But the nightmare of being alone: no way to breach that thick wall of silence that surrounds her. No one calls, she complains. But did you call them? No, she replies. Why not? She can't explain.

She confesses to her friend that she can't leave her husband because if she did, she'd float away. She confesses to her sister that if she left her husband she would die of isolation in an attic where the cats will be left to scavenge for themselves; she confesses here she can't leave him because she's terrified she will become antimatter, that event horizon of post-being.

Unconsciously aware that her centre of the world was nowhere, she became skilled at locating the centre of other people's universes and living there for a time; this behaviour was a rope attached to whomever, for a while. To kind of cave into the other's systems and live there. She faked it. Some call it parasite, or some mention fish. So ashamed to smell herself in her friend's eyes, so terrified of smelling her fishiness, her will unlatches and she sails off floating in 2001.

She was Goldilocks always trying on someone else's porridge for size, looking for her 'just right,' and even when she got it, she'd realize that these oats belonged to someone else and oh my, she had trespassed, this wasn't her house. Smell of overstaying the welcome anxiety, she'd take off, de-crossing the imaginary boundaries of property and attachment, while sacrificing the imaginary borders of love and rights. As you can imagine, navigating all the ley lines of other people's worlds exhausted her which is why she always looked like she wasn't doing anything. Maybe that's why, sometimes, they forgot she was there.

She had no way to explain what she was, why she was always on a rollercoaster, unable to keep her bearings, felt isolated, even among those she considered close. They converted her behaviour into their words. Their words fit fine, just fine. Anxiety, depressions. Oh, this is just adolescence. This will pass, you will move on and be someone brilliant. Oh, this is Saturn returning and soon it'll all be good. And of course, the life-fulfilling future never arrived. The good times eluded her. Trusting others defeated her.

She failed as a mother, if motherhood is about bonding and building trust. And ironically, as if her failure to bond needed to manifest in physical terms, she even failed to lactate and feed her child in the first 7 long agonizing days of his life. For the first several months she didn't believe that her son loved her. Put in perspective, her psychic issues were going haywire in this new set of problems: an infant is vulnerable and needy and she understood that; but somehow she was caught in not being seen by him. So she tried very hard to put aside her own vision and just be nurturing, giving. The outcome was that she learned about trust with him. He demanded what he wanted. No ulterior motives there. She trusted him.

But motherhood is not a cure for disorders, it merely postpones issues to another day.

3. PASSING NEUROTIC

As a 30 year old woman, she got her hands on the story of the ugly duckling looking for mom and was reminded of how it felt reading it as a kid. Such a satisfying story: everyone will find their people if they just keep looking. Sort of the promise that a prince shall come (one day). Everyone will find their home, finally. People who wanted her not as a substitute; a place that wouldn't disappear out from under her.

The BPD is defined by being neither neurotic nor psychotic. In fact, the BPD was a term that became necessary by practitioners to address diagnosing a patient who manifested both neurotic and mad tendencies. They are neither, but symptomatically, they are also both. The contradiction is what makes BPD the way they are and so hard to diagnose.

From the outside, she could pass as a neurotic, like anyone else and had managed to fool the psychiatric community for four decades. They took her at face value: no turbulence on her face in her eyes, so she was just fine. She could smile. But no one looks into the eyes. Like that time at the Clarke when, sitting beside her mother, the internationally recognized psychiatric pundit asked some benign questions with a smile on his face and, based on her reply, deduced there was "little wrong with her" that some talking therapy couldn't fix. "Everything would be fine," he said, reaching to pat her on the back: good dog. A gesture performed entirely for her mother's relief.

She went to one guy for years who may or may not have recognized she was BPD; whatever his diagnosis, he didn't share with her. He was supposed to be watching her, but it was the other way around. She wouldn't lie on the coach and instead faced him when talking; within minutes, he was asleep. It wasn't unusual, since another therapist she had once had when she was

14 used to fall asleep. But that therapist had an illness, whereas this therapist... Once the BPD even caused the pen in his hand to fall to the floor, making a pluncting noise that startled him awake. Embarrassing. Embarrassed, she pretended to ignore it and continued droning on.

She married, raised a child, and today has a home. But to be fair to all, none of this feels stable for her. It is a rug that can be pulled out from under. She has passed through the cracks of the institution and compensated by faking it, becoming a high functioning BPD.

4. PARANOIA

She's convinced her paranoia serves her. She's paranoid that her dearest friend had suspected who she was all those years ago. No clue really what BPD was that day she sat there across from her dearest friend trashing the BPD interfering in her friend's life. Manipulative, destructive and invasive. Disgusted with that person spreading her toxicity with the man who happened to be her dear friend's lover. It was exhausting, her dearest friend said. What a train wreck on feet, the BPD added. And the BPD looked at her friend as if for affirmation and her friend affirmed yes, but there was this second look in her friend's eye. Was her dearest friend considering her friend was BPD? And in her own words, this BPD was diagnosing herself, a train wreck on feet.

Yes, obviously her dear friend, dealing with one BPD, saw parallels with her friend, at that stage undiagnosed. The BPD noted strange moments of tension between them, after all. Her friend's withdrawal. Or peevishness. Most notable was that yawn that laced their daily meet-ups, as if the oxygen had been sucked from the air. As if the BPD was the black hole that was psychically crushing the atmosphere. A dense gravity of a need so profound no language could navigate around it; no rope strong enough to haul her back to humanity.

Oh, such melodrama!

This BPD had somehow figured out early that she needed to stop exhausting people, if she was going to be included: if this world doesn't want to know "about it" she had to keep her mouth shut. Be a good patient by having patience and returning daily and talking to herself, because the analyst needs to make a living and he is tired. Pretend to do therapy. Pretend not to notice how he sleeps. Manipulate with a conscience. Do something so her friend is not afflicted with her need. Make a joke about anything and then turn attention on her good friend. How's the writing going?

She let the therapist doze as she droned out her patterns of narrative in the air, much like planes do when drawing messages for Sally or Sue (marry me, already!) Impressed by how she could fashion stories of all parts of her life with almost nothing: some gasoline and the blue wide yonder. Or a little stove and some sour dough and you have leavened the bread of another inexplicable failure. Each telling kneading the hero who struggles against the beast of betrayal. This high-wire balance always in the back of her mind, not quite seeing but suspecting that her mantra "why is everything so difficult?" is a symptom. But she didn't know about symptoms then. So self-absorbed, she could barely question why everyone seemed to sail through things she found abhorrent such as schmoozing and performing, or impossible to navigate, such as more schmoozing. So much was also a mystery to her. For example, when someone looked at her with that question in the eye, was it a hidden signal of contempt? For example, if someone made a joke with a smile, were they masquerading their disgust with her? Or secretly sure she's a chickenhead. For example, if she was not offered the job, it was because she knew they believed her to be incompetent. Paranoid thinking.

Her friend yawns, and that's the sign that BPD is sucking all the oxygen from the air, so she turns to her friend asking about her date and her friend comes back to life waxing about what a brilliant night. And for the afternoon, this BPD is happy to live inside the joy of her friend's life.

Walking home, her inner world comes crashing back. This golem she has built out of yeast and terror. The better to defend myself, she says to herself. Exhausting to live with herself. Live in someone else's universe, why not? Or bridge the divide and make a joke about how terrible life is and at all costs, hide the volcano raging with paranoia, anxiety thundering around her. A train wreck on feet. Sometimes the horror drowns out all other noises, so she stands there looking like the chickenhead she thinks they think she is.

It is true, life went on for three more decades with that question, what is wrong with me? Coming back between forays into other people's worlds. The envy in seeing the swan find her home while countless tsunami crises hit her from all sides and from anyone, the boss, the acquaintance, the girlfriend of a colleague. Always so much happening inside about the outside: so much sliding into the imaginary and being yanked back by the real of profound confusion. Talking it through did help, it did. She'd come up with another narrative and in all this narrativizing, this poking and threading and slashing and constructing, she could see that nothing in the world was real. She is not real, fake as she is.

The BPD, such as Lady Diana, does not respect borders and tramples across the daisies, bangs into the rose bush. Except this BPD is such a shrinking violet, that the only borders she will trample are inanimate or those closest to her. She will abuse them with her neediness at 5 am, 3 am, 9 until forever. She will lash out with raging invectives at all but her son. Or, at least, she did everything she could to protect her son from herself, but even then, as her sister reminded her, there was a day she pushed her son away "Get away!" on his birthday.

5. FAILURE

The people closest to her see her inner ugliness, they forgive her. Why they do is a mystery to her. But to everyone else, she has hidden things "good." She has spent so many years ordering this anxiety around her words, demanding this body and its DNA and their red imaginary lines conform so that she would be accepted as everyone else, that she is accepted, she thinks. Shaping her body so she would fulfill their desires; trying to figure out their desires; shaping her mind to emulate the best. And then the carpal tunnel of the will sets in, she falls away in failures and floats until she's found another universe in her 2001 drift.

In all cases, she feared she was being exposed as a fraud. Or this is just melodrama, just indulging in her Cobain grunge, all metaphor on her hypersensitivity, another badly designed Golem coming off her back—oh, what else, oh almost anything that proved she was just looking for attention.

Shut the fuck up.

She spent years shutting it down, more dough and terrifying anger, and hiding it, the texture of her neediness, the maroon shade of it, so that she was confused when she saw that expression on someone's face, not many, but some. "What do you want from me?" in that body posture of a teacher, looking sideways and annoyed. As if there was something ravenous reaching from her face, the cloying perfume of a dying animal seeking repair, or the malformed product of a mother's ungiven milk unconsciously expressing the hunger of addiction. So much disgust in that expression "what do you want from me?" So much ickiness: ooh, get off of me.

Their discomfort was evidence that she just didn't belong, as if she were poaching on their land. In those circumstances, of which there were many, she would run away from the porridge she failed to make her own and reach for another paradigm for living. She left the city and pretended to be a small town scholar at a cozy university. She left the country and pretended to be a seamstress in a sweat shop. She pretended to be a starving poet. She left and started over again in the film industry. She left the city and pretended to be a writer. She left the country and pretended to be a European teacher of English as a Second Language. She returned pretending to be a mother. Returned to university and pretended to be a scholar.

The pretence of being something new is exhausting, which is why, years ago now, she had a wish that she could just be allowed to step off the planet. She was so alone, so isolated. And the reasons revolved around a future all mapped out around Kubrick's *Space Odyssey*. Just Louis XVI furniture, a chair and table, that god-awful bed, and those meals that appeared out of nowhere. This life of isolation caused by the destiny defined by the planets, the stars. There was no place in this deterministic, silent and lonely life where she could sit and rest among 'her people.' She had no people.

Even with family now, there is isolation. It is a terrible contradiction, suffering this and compensated only at times when she had entered her son's world and its wonders. Reliving her own childhood. Well, the son has become a man who lives far away, and with all her heart she is broken by his absence. But he's got a life and she hopes not ruined by her behaviour during his growing years. She lives with the man whom she loves. Who would have been better off with someone else, she thinks.

She was doomed to fail in finding "her kind," an ugly duckling grown into some deformed thing that she hid at all costs because revealing her monstrosity would mean being abandoned once and for all. Imagine how much energy is required to hold to this confession. To hold it straight so you can read between the lines; to hold the words to the meaning they claim.

6. FURIOUS

In therapy, she listened to her mind talking to itself and when she realized she was not only really good at fictionalizing to justify her "hurt feelings," aka ineluctable betrayals/demands that had to be accepted at all costs, she was also really good at hiding the Jupiter storms inside her. Forget those moments of Martian paranoia that overwhelmed her more severely than PMS cramps. In terms of Mercury, she wore the childish wig of the girl on the oatmeal hunt, hiding her beast genes from the camera. Put your flesh back on, please. Oh, she wished she could be Botticelli's Venus and not care what others thought.

She always walked away from the analyst's couch with her costume partly slipping off, satisfied that psychiatry hadn't found her. It was a kind of excruciating satisfaction: yet again, not seen. Not one of them saw it, not even when disorder slipped in through her verbs, her narratives. Her great castles of self-loathing. Not one caught that border where she always suspected she hovered, between neuroses and psychosis. In retrospect, maybe there was no care. Unless she fooled them all because she's really good at poker. Not. Unless they didn't want to look too closely, because it would mean having to rethink the therapy.

Her therapist should have been someone to talk to. The fact is, she was spinning her wheels by droning on and on. The buzzing like flies that put the analyst dead asleep till the session was up. It never occurred to her she could fire the analyst. That she deserved therapy.

She had no idea what kind of ugly duckling she was; she tried so hard to keep the dress code, marvelled at how easy it was for others, tried to fake it, and thought her anguish was a prolonged adolescence. Sort of like the Peter Pan syndrome. She waited for the day her mind would finally catch up to her body and fit; exhausted, she couldn't stay the course; she was a failure before starting. All talk of depression and anxiety was considered bunk since there were periods when she was perfectly fine. Just fine. Which reinforced the claim that her sickness was a pretense; that she was manipulative.

To be labeled drama queen. To be told to grow up.

When the ground shook and the windows started rattling because of profound betrayal and she was just waiting for the paranoic chatter of Mercury to rise into fever pitch, the BPD held tight, and waited to vent. From the outside, she looked calm, but when she talked the flat affect would come. She probably sounded as shallow as a puddle on the street. Not a shudder in reflecting the broad blue skies. How could she reveal her inner tectonic plates? How could she let her emotional ecosystem speak? Even now, she hesitates to admit how minor an event such as a student sighing in class can read 10 on the paranoid Richter scale as an indication of boredom. Or when a student gets up and walks out. This is something that she still can't master. It takes all her energy to not collapse into a pool at the podium. Instead, her voice fades and shudders, she hyperventilates. Her whole body is a sink hole under everyone's watchful stare.

7. DESTROYER OF WORLDS

He never asked what happened that led her to admit herself: he never knew about her greatest secret because he never asked directly and she would never confess it voluntarily. That would make her look bad. The rages that overcame her. This was her secret. She did not talk about cutting, or self-harm; it was a secret, in the quiet of her own room. She never shared anything about her destructiveness. She kept it from everyone, except her mother. Who saw it all and tried everything she could to stop it.

She had many invisible ways of being destructive. She did not eat. She spent years not eating which passed, unseen by others. Which is not unusual: people tend to miss the 'lack' of things. Oh, did you lose some weight? You look great! As if underweight is the symptom of vanity. As if the work she had done, the psychic sculpting to cut out the fury, came across as far more delicate than she felt it. When she shrank her world to herself alone, there was no one left to notice how little of her was left. Except, eventually, her sister looked.

The day she knew she needed something more than the Valium her mother was pushing on her, was the day she had trashed every little object of her dear life. As if the object contained all the trauma and suffering. As if the object, once pulverized, would erase the cause of this moment. As if all these little items of life, the little angel gifted on a birthday, the stones collected, each pattern with a particular life meaning, the candle and the pens, the ruler, the stickies, were at fault for her failing to survive. All so satisfyingly reduced to dust mixed with a little sour blood. The desk was too big to destroy so she just smashed her fists on it and bruised herself and cut where she could. The desk remained, stained, but whole. In retrospect, it was a raft. Or it was an element of the world that would not succumb to her "drama." It was the ship that would get her to Jupiter. No, it was Jupiter, her future.

She is guilty of breaking things. It was her fault, after all. As punishment, she drew blood, shed muscle, erased and erased and was a destroyer of worlds. The desk, the place where she invented herself, was so massive in her psyche, it was a planet on which she could carve her confession. She did. She literally used a pen to dig into the wood.

The closest the analyst got to recognizing her for what she was, was his comment that fall day: "you seem to hold contradiction inside yourself." No shit, Sherlock.

Oh, the psychiatrist had no idea how that contradiction, the dialectic, made her look unstable to everyone around her. Her impulsive moves, of which there were many, were ill thought actions to counter malaise, or stasis, or yet another failure. More than that, because she couldn't tell the psychiatrist about rage, he couldn't see her truth: that the destruction of beautiful things proved that she knew life was fiction. What animates us through the physical world? The delusion that our anchors tell us who we are. She knew that all of it was pure lead, thick with meaninglessness.

It goes without saying she has written reams and reams and what she has to show for this writing are crumbs. Little bits left over from her pulverizing disorder.

So much creation and so little to show for it. So much life in every breath and no one there to witness it.

Except Jupiter, her gravity. Even if it has no sentience, Jupiter doesn't erase her.

8. ERASURE

Turning back to see her tracks, she is shocked by how chaotic her progress, arriving at this moment on the gps that signals a wide circle.

Her roads circle the fact that her destiny is to revolve around nothing. She is pure circumference and always, always constructing some forward path, spinning on herself. Just another fruitless universe. A life so hollow no one notices she's there; so not there that the photographer in that photo of the crew and actors for the film, had documented her face in the crowd as some flesh beneath the leafy bush. Talk about erased.

In response to the analyst's query about whether she felt empty she replied: No, I don't feel empty; I feel disappeared.

She has had to ask for this assessment of her disorder not to find herself; no, rather, she is going into it to look into the eyes of an industry with its BLUE DSMs from one to five, that has overlooked her for over four decades. And she'd like someone in the psychiatric community to see what she feels. Well, the truth is, it was her sister who had already seen it, fed up with the endless hours trying to coach her out of bad thinking, so had given her the list of symptoms and they went through it together and yes, this BPD said yes to each one. Which is why this BPD asked for an assessment. She didn't need to be told who she was.

Oh, but the relief to see herself being seen, for once.

Perhaps her feeling of being erased originates with her mother's interpretation of her behaviour, continually reading her symptoms as everything but, even though it's 3 am and this BPD has her on the phone, in extreme crisis.

Her mother doesn't agree with the psychiatrist's assessment. "Well, I wouldn't go so far as to say that." "But why not?" "There are many reasons for your behaviour." "Yes, but the psychiatrist diagnosed me." "You need to get a proper diagnosis."

The rage that flares up as a bomb in her body which forces her to abruptly end the call with her mother and stew all day.

9. MAGICAL THINKING

When she was five, her mother brought her to see Kubrick's *2001: A Space Odyssey* in a huge theatre. The girl believed travelling to Jupiter was real and was disturbed by the fact that when we got there we would become very old and completely alone, served food by invisible hands in a white room surrounded by a clinical silence. So young, she was terrified by this accelerated aging.

Imagine pulling away the folds of this woolly thinking to reveal the ugly duckling, an old woman, long ago abandoned, caught in the gravity of a monstrous desire. She is just a girl in Kubrick's Jupiter, asking a question. This ugly duckling. Oh, my little one, let me take you home.

SUBJECTIVE DESTITUTION

Float not
a good float, but stuck
in the soiled

bed where dreams lake
you, subject
you to eddies of long shredded

youth. all you want is to leaf
or reed this stinking patch, a briar of chaos
branches, breached, and you'd be through

with limbs; wave, bend, toss
the salad of you
twisting, upside down

spoiled dreams of you
as quilted need, heavy
water, holding you

from bolting for the fence
with the offensive
question: is this horror

nature or
lack of nurture?

fuck this don't
even think it

that hand
to reach down
and pull the plug

pull the tooth
from the wrong mouth

bad words all
in the horseshoe of this
poem

Notes and Acknowledgements

This project came together retroactively. I had been writing these pieces to document experience, frustration, rawness, daily trouble and their scabs. The diagnosis changed my perspective on what I'd been doing and highlighted for me what I'm calling the product of a high functioning BPD: some pieces pretend to be 'normal' and other pieces struggle with 'normal,' and underlying this is the child playing against the brick wall of 'normal.' It is thanks to Shane Neilson, who has been supporting my work for several years now, that this project of an atypical, 'a-normal' life has an audience. I am so very grateful and indebted to Shane for creating this forum for disabilities discussion in which I, among others, may have a published voice.

Thanks to my family and my friends, always, for being there, having my back, especially in my difficulties, and for forgiving me.

Thanks to *Wordgathering* for publishing an earlier version of "Letter to the Future Without Snow"; Thanks to *The Antigonish Review* for publishing an earlier version of "Blue;" and thanks to *Eastern Iowa Review* for publishing "Where Are."

Thanks to the Ontario Arts Council Recommenders Grants and to Hamilton Arts and Literature for their support in this project in earlier stages.

About the Author

Concetta Principe is an award-winning poet, and writer of creative non-fiction, short fiction, as well as scholarship that focuses on trauma literature. *Discipline N.V.: A Lyric Dictionary*, has just come out with Palimpsest Press (2023.) Her first poetry collection, *Interference* (1999) with Guernica Editions, won the Bressani Award for poetry in 2000. Her poetry collection, *This Real*, published by Pedlar Press, was long-listed for the Raymond Souster Award in 2017. She teaches at Trent University.